WALKS AROUND CLITHEROE

10 WALKS UNDER 7 MILES

Dalesman

First published in 2006 by Dalesman
an imprint of
Country Publications Ltd
The Water Mill
Broughton Hall
Skipton
North Yorkshire BD23 3AG

First Edition 2006

Cover: below Pendle Hill by Terry Marsh

A British Library Cataloguing-in-Publication record
is available for this book

ISBN 1 85568 229 X

Printed by Compass Press Ltd

PUBLISHER'S NOTE
....
The information given in this book has been provided in good faith and is intended only
as a general guide. Whilst all reasonable efforts have been made to ensure that details
were correct at the time of publication, the author and Country Publications Ltd
cannot accept any responsibility for inaccuracies. It is the responsibility of individuals
undertaking outdoor activities to approach the activity with caution and, especially if
inexperienced, to do so under appropriate supervision. The activity described in this book
is strenuous and individuals should ensure that they are suitably fit before embarking
upon it. They should carry the appropriate equipment and maps, be properly clothed and
have adequate footwear. They should also take note of weather conditions and forecasts,
and leave notice of their intended route and estimated time of return.

Contents

Introduction

The area around Clitheroe is steeped in mystery and tales of witchcraft, which simply adds intrigue to many of the walks in this book. But the Pendle countryside also forms part of the Forest of Bowland Area of Outstanding Natural Beauty, and deservedly so.

The whaleback shape of Pendle Hill is a dominant and well-known landmark, and the River Ribble that flows through the middle is equally renowned for its flora and fauna, and excellent walking. It is quite a delight to wander the banks of the Ribble in summer when the sand martins have returned and are busy breeding in the river banks. Goosander, dipper, grey heron and kingfisher are present throughout the year, but don't be surprised to see a darting sparrowhawk, a kestrel or merlin on any of these walks. And the more remote the walk, the greater the likelihood of spotting little owls, or maybe a spectacular short-eared owl quartering the heathery moorland slopes of Bradford Fell.

At one extreme, this beautiful landscape offers you riverside walking as good as any, whether you stroll beside the Ribble, or do the Whalley walk (no 5), which will bring an acquaintance with the River Calder. Elsewhere, there are streams and brooks that sparkle and entertain as they thread a way through a surprisingly undulating setting.

Maybe without anyone realising it, the village of Downham is one of the best known in Lancashire, featuring as it does in the television series *Born and Bred*, as, indeed, it did in the 1961 film *Whistle down the Wind*, starring Hayley Mills and Alan Bates. But there are more lovely villages to be explored. Bolton-by-Bowland, which has some outstanding vernacular architecture and a lovely medieval church; Whalley, with its abbey; Sawley, likewise; West Bradford, Chatburn, Sabden, Barley, Hurst Green, Grindleton and Waddington, all small, comely settlements with great appeal, an appeal that is typical of this dazzling part of Lancashire walking country.

None of the walks in this book are excessively demanding, but you should approach them with caution if you are inexperienced. Always wear boots and appropriate clothing, and carry the relevant Ordnance Survey map.

Sawley and the Ribble

Distance: 5 miles (8 km)
Time: 2¹/₂ hours
Terrain: mainly field and riverside paths, sometimes wet
and muddy
Start/Finish: Sawley (or Chatburn), grid ref 776466
Map: Explorer OL41 (Forest of Bowland & Ribblesdale)

An agreeable and easy walk that visits an ancient abbey and spends a good deal of time in the delightful company of the River Ribble.

Sawley Abbey is well worth a visit. This Cistercian abbey was founded in 1148, but was affected by the Dissolution of the Monasteries in the sixteenth century. The monks were put back in the abbey during the subsequent Pilgrimage of Grace, and they stayed there until the uprising collapsed, when the abbot and two monks paid for their insurrection with their lives.

Start off down the road parallel with the River Ribble, which is crossed at Sawley Bridge. Across the bridge, immediately turn left over a stile onto a riverside path that rejoins the road a little further on. Turn left and follow the road for almost half a mile, as far as a footpath sign on the left just where the road bends to the right.

Leave the road here, and take to a path across a field leading to a step-stile in a corner. The on-going path curves across the top of a slope and then drops to a ladder-stile at the bottom of the field. Cross this and go right. Cross a stream and then immediately bear left beside it. A short way on, as you reach the Ribble, turn right and follow a fence until it meets a wall. Cross a stile and the corner of another field to rejoin the riverbank. Now keep following the river until a stile puts you onto a path that shortcuts a bend in the river, rejoining the riverbank at another stile.

Keep on along the embankment until you reach a road and bridge south of Grindleton. Turn left, cross the bridge and follow the road until it bends right. Here, leave it over a stile beside a gate (ignore a broad track) and bear left to return to the riverbank. The path leads back to join the broad track at a gate and stile.

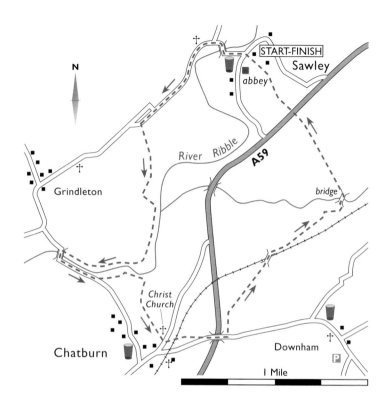

Walk along a concrete-surfaced track to a footbridge. Once over this, the path bears away from the river, passes through a kissing-gate and then along the top edge of a rough pasture. Later, continue up-field, targeting the steeple of Christ Church. After a gate, go along the edge of a school playing field to the main road in Chatburn.

Cross into Ribblesdale View opposite, climbing gently. At the top, bear left along Chatburn Road. Cross the bridge high above the A59. Immediately, turn left opposite a footpath sign (on the right). Cross a stile to follow a track that later swings right along a field boundary. Eventually, you arrive at a kissing-gate. This leads onto an enclosed path which goes on to cross a railway bridge. The path then bears right and runs out to enter a field. Keep along the field edge and soon reach a barn.

Pass through a gap just after the barn, and go forward alongside a wall bordering a large pasture. When the wall changes direction, continue to follow the field edge, now alongside a fence, to a step-stile. Beyond this, a path runs beside a hawthorn and hazel hedgerow, and drops to a footbridge in the bottom corner of the field. From the bridge, cross the middle of the ensuing field, following an indistinct grassy path. On the far side of the field, descend to a through-stile

The dipper is often to be seen near fast-flowing rivers and streams.

in a corner. Cross the lovely single-arch bridge nearby. This featured in the television series *Born and Bred*, much of which was filmed in and around Downham.

Cross a stile and climb left up to a step-stile on the skyline. From this, head up a large field, making for a step-stile a few strides to the right of the field corner. Go down the right-hand edge of the next field to another corner stile. Cross to a metal gate before heading down the ensuing field to the A59.

Taking care as you cross the road, pass through a kissing-gate opposite. Walk down-field to another kissing-gate. From here, head down an old sunken lane, often overgrown, that leads to the edge of woodland. At the bottom, cross a narrow lane and go through a kissing-gate to a stile to the left of a gate. Now descend half-left to a stile giving into a car park opposite the Spread Eagle Hotel to complete the walk.

Pendle Hill from Barley

Distance: 4¹/₄ miles (7 km)
Time: 2¹/₂ hours
Terrain: generally good paths throughout, but the top of Pendle Hill is confusing in poor visibility
Start/Finish: main visitors' car park in Barley, grid ref 823402
Map: Explorer OL41 (Forest of Bowland & Ribblesdale)

With quite a steady pull to the top of Pendle Hill, this walk is no pushover, but the views are well worth the effort. Poor visibility makes the top of the fell potentially confusing, and such days are best avoided.

Leave the car park along a surfaced path across a playing field that leads to a roadside path. When you emerge onto the road, pass the Barley Mow Restaurant and the Barley Village Tea Room. Then, a little further on, leave the road by turning left at Meadow Bank Farm onto a signposted footpath that courts a narrow stream.

From a kissing-gate, cross a rough pasture to a footbridge and then a narrow lane. Turn left along the lane. Pass a large cottage and branch right at a metal

The stoat is commonly found in hedgerows, farmland and wooded areas, though it is not always easy to spot despite its distinctive brown coat with white underparts.

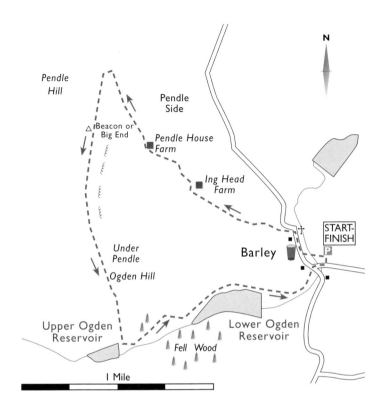

kissing-gate onto a cobbled path, part of the Pendle Way. The path later becomes gravelled and enclosed for a while, and leads to a kissing-gate. From here, walk alongside a fence and later a wall as you head up to reach Brown House.

Pass Brown House and through a gate onto a wide track near Ing Head Farm. Follow the track briefly, then turn left through another gate. A gravel path rises beside a wall to another gate and a clear on-going path rising steadily to Pendle House Farm.

At Pendle House, go through a gate and turn right along the farm boundary. Shortly, bear left to another gate at a wall corner. Here, a stepped path begins the ascent of Pendle Hill. The 'pull' is not so bad as might seem, and a steady plod with frequent rests will soon bring you to the edge of the summit plateau, a vast, sprawling, largely featureless moorland.

At the top of the path, turn left beside a wall, but continue only as far as a wall corner and ladder-stile. From here, strike across rough moorland to the trig pillar that marks the summit. This is the highest point for some distance, providing lovely views over Ribblesdale, to the Yorkshire peaks and as far as the fells of Lakeland.

From the trig point, stay roughly parallel with the escarpment edge, heading south, and passing two large piles of stones. Lower down, you cross the head of an alternative line of ascent. Keep following the escarpment until it reduces to no more than a grassy slope. Then, simply keep on descending in the same direction, following a peaty path that becomes narrower, until it finally drops to meet a step-stile at the head of a sunken track.

Lapwings are still a common sight round Pendle Hill.

Go through a field gate. Descend the left-hand edge of a rough pasture, following a wall. Lower down, cross a farm track. Keep descending, more steeply now, to the service track for Upper Ogden Reservoir at a gate. Turn left along the track.

Eventually the track becomes surfaced and runs down to the edge of Lower Ogden Reservoir. Keep following the track, past the reservoir. Eventually you will reach the edge of Barley. Cross into the road opposite to return to the car park.

Sabden and Spence Moor

Distance: 5¹/₂ miles (9 km)
Time: 3 hours
Terrain: generally good paths, occasionally indistinct on the moors
Start/Finish: Sabden village car park, grid ref 778373
Maps: Explorer OL21 (South Pennines) and
Explorer 287 (West Pennine Moors)

Spence Moor above the village of Sabden is quite a delight at any time of year; frozen conditions make for easier walking in winter. The view of the moorlands of eastern Lancashire, above Colne and Nelson, is excellent.

Leave the car park and turn left up the main street. Turn right into Wesley Street, and walk up towards the parish church. On reaching the church, go left up the lane to Badger Wells Cottages. Continue round bends and up to a T-junction. Here, go left to cross the stream of Churn Clough, following the lane as it climbs to the right to reach the end of the terraced Badger Wells Cottages.

Pass to the right of the cottages to follow a sunken pathway, ascending easily to a gate. Beyond, a green path runs on to another gate, at which you leave the field to parallel Badger Wells Water.

Continue with the path as it rises easily, reaching the open fellside at a wall and gate. The on-going path climbs steadily to meet an east-west track. Turn right along it. Cross the top end of a field, before continuing once more above the intake wall with Churn Clough Reservoir in view below.

A short way on, the rocky outcrop of Deerstones appears. As it does, ignore a branching track on the left. Keep on to descend across a stream-filled gully. Once across the stream, the track rises a little and degenerates into a narrow path as it approaches a larch plantation.

Follow the top edge of the plantation and descend to cross another stream. Ignore a stile into the plantation, and instead rise left on a peaty path through bracken below Deerstones. At the top edge of the plantation, keep forward, rising steadily on a clear path that soon escapes the bracken and peat to take

11

a grassy course, gradually approaching and then swinging round above Deerstones.

On reaching the path above Deerstones, you can simply stroll, right, onto the tussocky top before continuing to a wall and a parallel path. The path leads to a stile. Beyond, an initially wet continuation moves out onto Spence Moor, bringing Pendle Hill into view beyond Ogden Clough. The path continues south-east and descends obliquely to meet a wall at a stile.

Across the wall, a path trails indistinctly down through boggy moorland, roughly following a shallow sunken track. At a gate at the bottom of the hill, a path branches left for Newchurch-in-Pendle. Ignore this and keep ahead. Descend to reach the ruins of an old barn, of which only one gable remains.

Pass below the gable and head for a through-stile beside a gate at the top edge of Cock Clough Plantation. Cross the stile. Keep to the edge of the

The plaintive 'pee-oo' call of the golden plover is a distinctive sound heard on upland areas such as Spence Moor.

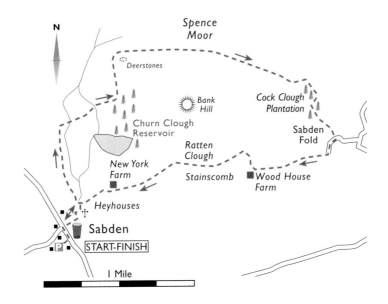

plantation, on a descending path, until the wall gives way to a short stretch of wire fence. Access Cock Clough at a simple stile just after the wire fence begins. Once in the clough, initially follow its upper boundary As the boundary wall changes direction, descend a broad wedge of ground that drops to a confluence of streams. An improving path then goes on down to the bottom of the clough.

As you reach the bottom, bear left to a simple stile over a fence. Go down a track to enter a corner of a farmyard, and walk ahead to a surfaced lane. Turn right, walking down the lane for a short distance. Bear right with it to pass Lower Lane Farm, where the lane becomes a cobbled track.

The track continues to Wood House Farm. It immediately fords a shallow stream, and shortly swings right to rise easily to Stainscomb, a fine Tudor farmstead with mullioned windows. At Stainscomb, the track, now surfaced again, swings up and left to begin an easy and level promenade, bound for the next farm, Ratten Clough. Go through the farmyard here. Simply follow a surfaced lane, at first across open fields and then flanked by thorn and holly, to arrive at New York Farm. From here, a narrow hedgerowed lane runs down to rejoin the outward route at Heyhouses. Turn left, and retrace your steps to the car park.

Hurst Green & the Ribble

Distance: 6½ miles (10.5 km)
Time: 3 hours
Terrain: generally good paths throughout
Start/Finish: Hurst Green, grid ref 685379
Maps: Explorer 287 (West Pennine Moors)

The area around Stonyhurst College has long been associated with Lord of the Rings *author J R R Tolkien, who is known to have stayed in the area while writing the book. Who knows, perhaps Hurst Green became Hobbiton, and the Ribblesdale countryside became the Shire?*

Begin by walking to the left of the Shireburn Arms to locate a stile below the main car park. Go down the edge of the ensuing field. When you can, move to the right of a small stream, and follow it to some duckboards and a footbridge. After a slight rise, wooden steps wind down to another footbridge just before the River Ribble. Bear left just above the river.

Cromwells Bridge is visible just downstream from Lower Hodder Bridge. The bridge was built in the sixteenth century by Sir Richard Shireburn.

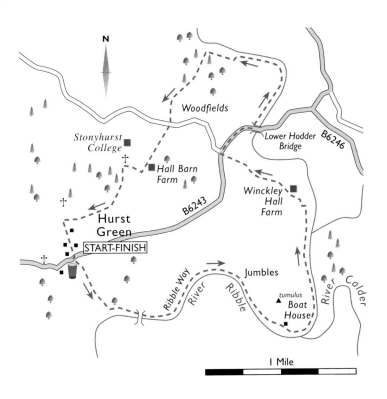

Skirt an aqueduct and return to the riverbank. Shortly, continue along a gravel track that later swings right past Jumbles. Stay on the track heading for the isolated Boat House. There, bear right (no discernible path) to rejoin the riverbank.

After rounding a big bend, go up slightly to a track. Follow this for about half a mile, until, opposite the confluence of the Ribble and the Hodder, you can keep forward through a gate.

Continue along the track to Winckley Hall Farm. There, go left towards houses, passing right, between barns, then left past a pond and out into a lane. This climbs steadily, and levels out, swinging left as it passes Winckley Hall. Go through a kissing-gate on the right and across the field to another. Keep straight on across a large field, keeping left of woodland. Descend to pass a pond and walk out to meet a road.

The wren is one of our most common and widespread birds, and is found wherever there is low cover such as hedgerows, scrubland and gardens.

Turn right down a roadside footpath to the river. Immediately before the roadbridge, branch left along a track. Follow the river, and then ascend past Hodder Place, before dropping to a bridge over a stream.

Go left along a wooded track, cross a footbridge, then climb a long flight of steps. Follow the top edge of a plantation, to a stile leading into a field. Keep to its edge. At the end, cross a stile into a stony track. Keep left, to pass Woodfields (where Tolkien is said to have stayed) and out to the road. Go down the track to Hall Barn Farm and along the right side of farm buildings.

Turn right on a surfaced track for 200 yards. Go left through a gate by the end of a wall. Continue along the left-hand side of a narrow field, but gradually bearing right to a path alongside a woodland boundary, that leads up to a kissing-gate. Follow the ensuing field edge to another kissing-gate.

At the top of the final field, go through a gate and onto a narrow path leading out to a short lane. At its end, turn left back to the start.

Whalley and its abbey

Distance: 6 miles (9.5 km)
Time: 3 hours
Terrain: good paths throughout; some road walking
Start/Finish: Whalley town centre, grid ref 733362; or Spring
Wood car park on A671, grid ref 741360
Map: Explorer 287 (West Pennine Moors)

It is only when you walk onto the surrounding hillsides above the town of
Whalley that you realise how beautiful the landscape around the River
Calder really is. Save time to explore the abbey itself, or to have a cuppa in
its Cloisters Coffee Shop.

Leave the centre of Whalley by walking north along the main street to a small
roundabout at the end of Station Road. Here, turn right into Brookes Lane.

As you reach the end of the lane, it forks. Bear right, passing through a gate
onto a track alongside a stream. At a gate just before a compound housing
radio masts, bear right and cross a step-stile. Go left up a broad grassy track
alongside a woodland edge. The track climbs steadily and then, as it levels,
swings left to a step-stile above the A671. Spring Wood picnic area and car
park are directly opposite, and you could choose to start the walk from here.

Cross the road junction at the lights and turn right along the A-road. When,
shortly, you reach the side road for Sabden, turn left, climbing gently. Take
care against approaching traffic as the road has no verges. When the road
meets Portfield Lane, cross the end of the lane and a step-stile opposite to
gain a large pasture. Bear slightly right of centre and then, as the pasture
slopes down towards a fence, head for another step-stile that appears below.

Cross the next field to a stile beside a gate, then head up to a stile/gate on
the skyline. Over this, keep on in much the same direction, passing around
the edge of a hollow. Descend to a stile in a corner, giving onto a surfaced
track. Turn left and walk out to a road.

Turn right and descend to cross Sabden Brook. On the other side, leave the
road by branching right through a gate onto a farm track (waymark). This

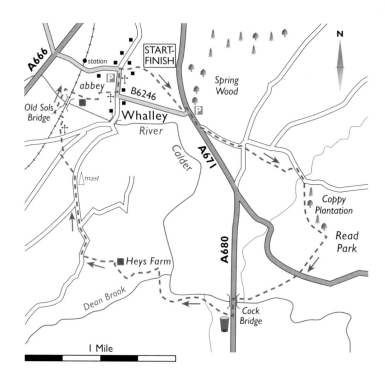

goes past a barn, and then along the boundary of Coppy Plantation into Read Park. Keep along the boundary to a gate. Just beyond, intercept a surfaced lane. Here, turn right and walk down the lane to meet the A671.

Cross the road with care. Go forward down a broad track opposite that leads down to meet the A680 beside the River Calder. Turn left for 200 yards. Just before reaching the first house on the right, cross a step-stile onto a path signposted for Whalley Nab. A grassy path leads on above the Calder, towards which it eventually descends. In the bottom corner of the field, cross a footbridge over an in-flowing stream, and continue beside the river.

In due course you encounter the gully of Egg Syke Brook. Cross, and climb the bank opposite, to walk above the Calder again to a kissing-gate in a corner. Beyond the gate, keep forward, high above the river. A short way further on, descend left through another gully and down steps to a ladder-stile and a slab bridge spanning Dean Brook.

Keep on for about 100 yards beyond the footbridge. Turn left, uphill, along a row of hawthorn and holly beside a sunken track (keep it on your right). At the top, cross a step-stile. Go forward along a woodland boundary to another stile. Over this bear left, still above the woodland edge, to arrive at Heys Farm.

Pass to the left of the farm buildings, and then ahead up a surfaced lane (Berry's Lane). At a T-junction you join a lane (Shaw-cliff Lane). Turn right and follow the lane for about three-quarters of a mile.

Yellow rattle (left) and cow-wheat are both yellow-flowering plants of summer meadows and heaths.

As you draw level with a radar mast, the lane begins to descend steeply. Continue downhill, passing the mast. Just before reaching the entrance to Wood Nook, leave the lane by climbing over a stile on the left, and going down-field alongside a reedy ditch on your right.

The bottom right-hand corner of the field is muddy, but here you will find a stile giving onto an enclosed path that descends to Whalley Old Road. Cross and go through a wall gap opposite, once more on an enclosed path. Descend to another road. Cross this diagonally right. Go down a path beside the Ebenezer Baptist Church onto a lane in front of cottages.

Keep descending past housing (Walmsley Brow) towards the viaduct, and you will reach a T-junction. Turn left and walk beneath the viaduct. Immediately turn right to walk beside it on a path enclosed by iron railings. This feeds you onto Old Sol's Bridge, spanning the Calder.

Over the bridge, walk out to meet a road. Turn right and go ahead through the fourteenth-century gatehouse of Whalley Abbey.

When you reach a school, Whalley Abbey and its coffee shop are to the right. The route continues to the left, passing the school, and then the Church of St Mary and All Saints. Keep forward to a T-junction in the centre of Whalley, to complete the walk.

Waddington

Distance: 4³/₄ miles (7.5 km)
Time: 2¹/₂ hours
Terrain: field and riverside paths, some road walking
Start/Finish: Waddington, grid ref 726435
Map: Explorer OL41 (Forest of Bowland & Ribblesdale)

Beginning in the delightful village of Waddington, this walk wanders country lanes to meet and follow the Ribble Way for a while as it heads for West Bradford. You can expect encounters with some strange wooden objects on this circular tour.

Start from a car park along Twister Lane, adjoining a children's play area and a sports pitch. Go along the lane, towards Waddington, and take the first turning on the right, signposted for Clitheroe and Mitton. Throughout this walk there are several sections of road walking, none of which has a roadside verge, so do take care against approaching traffic.

Continue past the turning to Clitheroe (Waddow View). Keep on for about three-quarters of a mile in all, until you can leave the road about 100 yards after the turning to Fields House Farm. Pass through a gate on the left, as the road bends to the right, and go forward along a field track that leads to Waddow Hall.

There is a waymarked route around the hall, now a Girl Guides training and activity centre. On the other side of the hall grounds, turn left along a surfaced track. Keep forward along this at a junction. A short way further on, as the main track bears left to meet a road, branch right on a narrower track to a gate giving onto the road just north of Brungerley Bridge.

Walk downhill to cross Brungerley Bridge. Leave the road by branching left through wrought-iron gates onto the Ribble Way, which here passes along a sculpture trail on the edge of Clitheroe. When the surfaced path divides, branch left towards the river.

Eventually, you leave the sculpture trail as the path runs on into Cross Hill Quarry Local Nature Reserve. Keep an eye open for a Ribble Way waymark

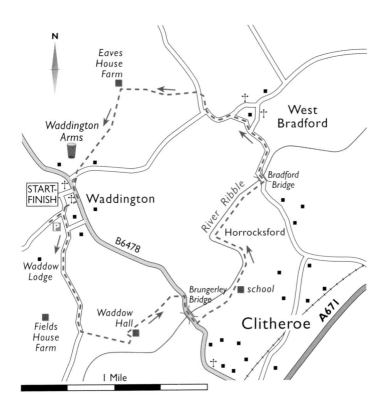

when the path next forks. Here branch left, descending towards the riverbank, reaching it at a gate. Continue forward beside a fence. Follow the Ribbleside path, later walking along an enclosed section to emerge onto a road at Bradford Bridge.

Turn left to cross the bridge, and follow the road all the way into the village of West Bradford, walking along Mill Street. At the top, at a T-junction, turn left towards the Three Millstones pub. Walk on past the pub. Take the next turning on the right, a byway that runs alongside a low wall and shortly passes the former Methodist graveyard. Just beyond, the track swings left and climbs to the road again. Turn right. After about forty yards, leave the road by branching left up steps at a footpath sign, and across the top of a small paddock to locate an old metal kissing-gate in a corner. The path continues around the edge of a small woodland. It then crosses an elongated field to a small footbridge spanning a stream, and a stile beyond.

In the next field, walk around the right-hand margin to a stile tucked in a corner. From the stile, head diagonally up the field, targeting Eaves House Farm. *(Waymarks at the stile are confusing, and suggest that you can walk around the field margin. While there is indeed a path, there is no right-of-way; the correct line is across the field.)*

Cross a stile directly in front of Eaves House and turn left. Walk down an access lane, but only as far as the turning on the right to the Stables. Here, on the junction, cross a step-stile to the left of a gate. Head down the middle of the ensuing field, to locate a footbridge in a stream gully.

The reed bunting favours farmland and wetland habitats.

Climb out of the gully, and cross the corner of a sloping pasture, allowing the hedgerow on your left to guide you to the outskirts of Waddington. Continue until you reach a gate and stile in a corner. Over this, follow a broad track out to reach the edge of the village. Turn right at a road. As you reach the centre of the village, turn left towards the churches. Walk on past the Waddington Arms, the Country Kitchen Tea Room and Waddington Old Hall.

On reaching the war memorial, go through a metal gate and down to cross a stream on stepping stones. *(If the stepping stones are under water, backtrack and walk around the village roads.)* Go up steps and forward through a gate to cross a large enclosure. On the other side, turn left and follow the road round to return to the car park.

Great Mitton

Distance: 4¹/₂ miles (7 km)
Time: 2¹/₂ hours
Terrain: good paths throughout; some road walking
Start/Finish: Edisford Road car park, Clitheroe, grid ref 728414
Map: Explorer OL41 (Forest of Bowland & Ribblesdale)

The Ribble is a delightful companion throughout much of this walk which explores the countryside around the parish of Great Mitton.

Set off from the car park by walking along a footpath parallel with the road, which leads down to Edisford Bridge. Cross the bridge, and on the other side turn left into a riverside pasture. Go forward into this and look for a low step-stile on the right. Over this, climb left, eventually rising to a gate above. This leads onto a broad track going forward into a mixed plantation of birch and larch. At the far side of the plantation, pass through another gate and go left along the plantation boundary to rejoin the riverbank. Now simply follow the river until you are channelled into a corner (step-stile). From here, go ahead and up steps to reach a large field.

Across the field you'll see an isolated building. Aim to the right of this, and you will find a stile near a gate. Cross the stile, go through the gate, cross an access track, and turn left over another stile. Now you are walking alongside a stream at varying distances, but eventually following its course out into a field. Stay with the stream, and you will come to a bridge.

Cross this and the nearby stile. In the next field, bear gradually left towards the left-hand field boundary, a hedgerow that runs alongside Malkin Lane. Near a field corner you cross a stile to gain the end of Malkin Lane. Turn right and walk out to meet the road into Great Mitton (Church Lane). Turn left and walk up to pass the church. Arrive at a T-junction near the Hillcrest Tea Room.

Go left and, taking care against approaching traffic, follow the road to Mitton Bridge. Continue until, just after the Aspinall Arms, you can leave the road at a gate on the left. Follow the left-hand boundary of the ensuing field to a stile. Over this, go ahead alongside a fence above the Ribble to a kissing-gate. Keep on in the same direction to find a footbridge spanning a stream.

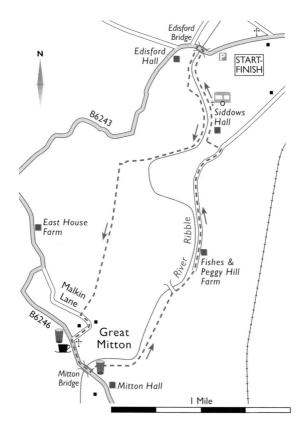

Over the footbridge, strike out across a large riverside pasture to an isolated building on the riverbank. Continue past this to join a surfaced track that runs past an aqueduct and on towards Shuttleworth Farm. Keep to the left of the farm buildings to locate a gate. Cross a small paddock to emerge on a road near Fishes and Peggy Hill Farm. Now simply follow the road (Henthorn Road) for about half a mile. Just after the end of a small woodland on the left, and after crossing a roadbridge spanning a stream, leave the road by turning left up a track. As it swings left, leave it by turning right along a surfaced access track, but soon leave this through a gate on the left.

Cross the next field, diagonally right, to find another gate. Join the riverbank once more. Now simply follow the riverbank back to Edisford Bridge, and there turn right to retrace your steps to the car park.

Bolton-by-Bowland

Distance: 4½ miles (7 km)
Time: 2½ hours
Terrain: field paths and ancient tracks, often wet and muddy;
some road walking
Start/Finish: Bolton-by-Bowland car park, grid ref 784493
Map: Explorer OL41 (Forest of Bowland & Ribblesdale)

Don't let the brevity of this walk lull you into thinking it's going to be a pushover. The farm fields, though most of them are trackless, are easy enough, but part of the route follows an ancient highway, maybe a packhorse trail, and here the going is quite energetic (and wet). In winter's frozen grip or on a balmy summer's day, this walk would be straightforward, but it's quite special at any time of year. Finally, the village of Bolton is a microcosm of vernacular architecture.

From the village car park, turn right along Main Street, and later keep on along the road for Gisburn, to pass the Church of St Peter and St Paul. If church architecture is your thing, then it's worth stopping off briefly to take a look at this venerable old building.

Just past the church, leave the road by turning right along the surfaced drive through Bolton Park. After a while the drive rises gently, with the remains of a cross just to the left of the high point. Keep forward, now descending. Just before a cattle grid, bear right onto a broad track around a park boundary. Go through a gate and continue along the boundary, then a fence, eventually to reach a footbridge spanning Skirden Beck.

Blackberries and rosehips are found in country hedgerows.

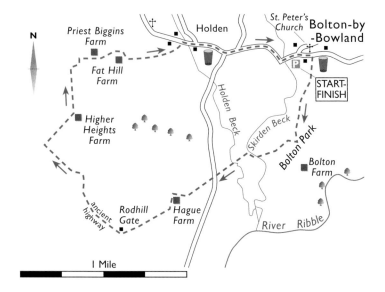

On the other side, bear right with a continuing track around a small wooded hillock. Follow the track to another footbridge across Holden Beck. Cross the bridge and bear right to rejoin the track. Walk up to meet the Sawley to Bolton road.

Cross the road and the step-stile opposite. Strike across the ensuing pasture, aiming for Hague Farm in the distance. By so doing you will discover a footbridge spanning Hell Syke, from which you should walk up towards the farm.

At the farm, go through a metal gate and turn left to pass through the farmyard. On the other side, as you start down the farm access track, leave it by passing through the first gate on the right. Keep on in the same direction to the far corner of the field. Cross a low step-stile. Keep climbing, maintaining the same direction.

When another farm (Rodhill Gate) comes into view, head towards it. Keep to the left of the farm to join an old track (Rodhill Lane). Turn right and cross a cattle grid. Continue up the lane until it swings left a short way further on. Here, leave it by passing through a gate onto a bridleway. This now ascends for some distance through a deep, wet and muddy gully. It may well be an ancient highway, possibly a packhorse trail, and in spite of its condition, deserves to be walked. But it is quite arduous, so expect an energetic few minutes before you break out at the top onto more level ground.

As the track levels, keep forward beside a fence towards a newish wooden gate. Pass to the left of the gate. You will see the ongoing track swinging left and climbing over a hill shoulder. The track leads up to a metal gate with a small stile to its right. Cross the stile and keep on beside a wall until you reach a broad, walled track at a T-junction.

Turn right and follow the track to Higher Heights Farm. Swing left to walk out along the surfaced farm access lane. Keep on down the lane. Just after a cattle grid, the lane swings right and then left. Continue for less than 100 yards, and look for a high through-stile in the wall on the right, at a wall corner. Clamber over this. Go forward alongside a wall and then a holly hedgerow to locate a step-stile. From this, descend to pass to the right of Priest Biggins Farm to another stile.

Go down the next field to a kissing-gate just above Fat Hill Farm. On passing to the left of the farm, bear right onto a track leading out to the farm access lane. Here, turn left and follow the lane down to a lower lane at the edge of Holden. Turn left and walk out to the village road, and turn right to pass through Holden to a T-junction.

Head for Bolton-by-Bowland now, with only road walking remaining — so do take care against approaching traffic. At a T-junction near the Copy Nook Hotel, go left and follow the road to Bolton to complete the walk.

Long-tailed tits colonise in woodland, hedgerows and heathland, and are recognisable by their stubby bodies and long tails.

Downham

Distance: 3 miles (5 km)
Time: 2 hours
Terrain: mainly field and riverside paths,
sometimes wet and muddy
Start/Finish: Downham, grid ref 784441
Map: Explorer OL41 (Forest of Bowland & Ribblesdale)

This lovely walk explores the undulating countryside around Downham. The convoluted nature of the landscape means that there are plenty of agreeable surprises in store as the route twists this way and that.

Begin from the car park near the information centre at the bottom of the village. Go through a gate and along a lane that curves round to meet the main village street. Turn left and walk up to the Assheton Arms.

Walk to the left of the pub, leaving the main road, and head along a surfaced lane between walls. Immediately after the last house, turn left through a gate and go up the edge of a pasture to an old form of squeeze stile. Continue alongside a boundary wall, climbing steadily. At the high point there is a waymark. From this bear right, out into a field, following — though there isn't much evidence of it — the course of a Roman road. Aim for woodland ahead. As you get nearer, move towards its right-hand edge, to walk alongside a fence to a stile.

Cross the stile and keep forward on a grassy path. Initially beside a fence, the path then keeps on in the same direction to a stone stile. Beyond this, press on along a hedgerow, following this across two fields to approach Hey House Farm.

As you near the farm, keep to the field boundary and walk around to a gap-stile about forty yards to the right of the farmhouse. From this, strike diagonally right across the next field to a stile beside a gate. Over the stile, go forward above an old quarry. Continue along a shallow sunken track that runs on beside a row of mature hawthorns and ash, and then beside a wall to a gap-stile. Cross the stile and maintain the same direction, passing three trees — an oak, a hawthorn and an ash. Head down towards Springs Farm.

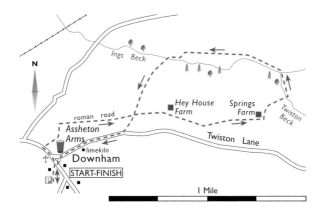

As you reach the farm, cross two step-stiles and then go left between the farm buildings across another stile directly in front of the farmhouse. Head down the left-hand edge of a sloping pasture to a footbridge at the bottom spanning Twiston Beck.

Over the bridge, go left beside the beck, which here runs through an area of light woodland. Soon you move away from the beck to another footbridge, this time across Ings Beck. Cross this, and again go left, soon passing the confluence between Ings and Twiston becks. Follow the combined becks until, at a fence, you are diverted away from them alongside the fence which steers you to a stile. Over the stile, and the immediate stream, head up-field on a grassy path. Once over the crest of the hill, you close in on a fenceline on the right. Follow this, descending a little, until you approach another gate (stile to the right, and not far from a farm) at the top of a steep slope.

Do not go through the gate, but descend steeply left, down to a stile over a fence. Cross to a nearby footbridge. Over the footbridge and the immediate fence, go uphill across the shoulder of a sloping field. The path leads to a squeeze stile in a corner. From it, keep on in the same direction across four more fields, crossing stiles to reach another on the skyline to the right of a solitary oak tree accompanied by a holly. Cross the stile, and a few strides further on you meet the outward route at a stone stile. Here you can turn right to retrace the first part of the walk.

Or go forward alongside a fence and eventually locate a gate in a corner through which you reach Twiston Lane. Turn right along the lane, which will take you back to Downham, and on the way passing an old lime kiln. You re-enter Downham near the post office and tea rooms. Turn left down the village road, and retrace your steps to the car park.

Bradford Fell

Distance: 6¹/₂ miles (10.5 km)
Time: 2¹/₂ hours
Terrain: Good tracks and paths, but some road walking
and pathless fields
Start/Finish: Grindleton, grid ref 758455
Map: Explorer OL41 (Forest of Bowland & Ribblesdale)

This walk to Bradford Fell is very much a walk on the wild side, and crosses heather moorland where you may well spot short-eared owls, deer, curlew and buzzard. The flowers in springtime make this walk a real pleasure.

There is only roadside parking in Grindleton. Once you have found a suitable parking spot, walk up the road beside the Duke of York pub (sign-posted for Harrop Fold). At the 'Top of Town', branch left into Whitehall Lane. Descend to cross Grindleton Brook before climbing to White Hall. In front of the hall, turn right, following the lane to Cob House Farm. Finally the surfaced lane ends and you go forward through a gate into a walled green lane.

At a second gate, you reach the top pasture. Go left over a stone stile. Start down the ensuing field, following a wall. When the wall changes direction, use a gate on the left to cross the continuing fence. Then go down the field on a grassy path beside a fence. At the bottom, cross a footbridge.

Over the bridge, bear left. Follow an initially indistinct path through rushes, passing the ruins of Simpshey Farm. Continue to climb easily to the top left-hand edge of bracken-clad Simpshey Hill ahead. The path meets a wall. Here, go left between walls, through a bridlegate and onto a rising path that curves round the end of the hill, eventually running parallel with a dilapidated wall. Take care: the wall layout here is a little confusing. The key to success, however, is the wall on your right, below the end of Simpshey Hill. So keep fairly close to this. At a corner you discover a broad path running almost northwards, heading for the plantation of Grindleton Forest.

This meets a rough-surfaced forest trail at a T-junction. Turn left and follow the trail, past the barely discernible remains of the farm at St Clare's. When

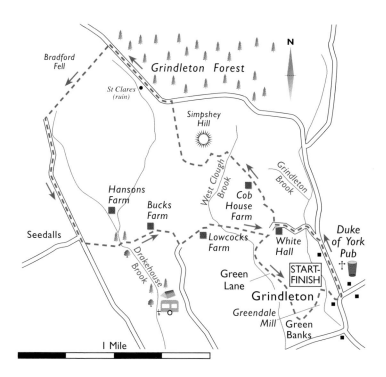

the trail finally swings right to a gate into the plantation, leave it by going forward through another gate and along a walled green lane.

A couple of hundred yards further on, at a junction, turn left onto another broad green track descending gently between walls. The track here crosses the lower slopes of Bradford Fell.

Eventually the track runs on to meet another, Moor Lane, at a T-junction. Turn left and go through a gate, and gently down the lane. Keep descending through lovely heather moorland to reach a barn on the left. Keep on past this, now descending with a fence on your left, as you go down beside a shallow holloway. The track finally comes down to meet a surfaced farm access. About eighty yards further on, leave the lane, left, for a bridleway crossing a cattle grid at the start of the track to Hansons Farm.

Immediately leave the farm track, striking obliquely right to the far right-hand corner of open pasture, heading for mixed woodland in the distance.

31

Very soon a gate comes into view. Aim for this. Go through the gate and slightly right, heading for a metal gate at the entrance to woodland that flanks Drakehouse Brook. Through the gate, go initially left and then right as you descend to cross the brook at a ford. Climb out on the other side. Walk along the edge of the woodland to locate a gate on the left. Walk the short distance across the next pasture and go through another gate. Continue beside a fence towards Bucks Farm.

As you approach Bucks Farm, go forward, keeping the farm buildings to your left, and you'll pass in front of the farmhouse to reach its access lane. Now follow this out, and stay with it as it swings right at a solitary gate pillar. Lower down, immediately after a cattle grid, turn left over another grid onto a track leading to Lowcocks Farm.

Go forward into the farmyard. On the other side, cross a stile beside a gate. Pass to the left of a water treatment works building, beside which a high wall is crossed by a stile. In the ensuing field, go ahead to reach the edge of woodland flanking West Clough Brook. Go down to cross the brook by a footbridge.

Keep forward to a metal gate, beyond which you briefly climb a sunken track. On level ground, go immediately right, across the field, roughly parallel with West Clough Brook, aiming for the farm buildings at White Hall.

A low stile takes you on across a fence corner. From it, keep on in the same direction across the next two fields, crossing fences by stiles. In the final field, head for the far left-hand corner. Leave it at a gate and stile.

Turn right, and walk past farm buildings to enter woodland and set off down an old track (Green Lane). Now simply follow this delightful, if muddy, lane as far as Green Banks, where the road bends left and immediately right. As it goes right, leave it, left, by crossing a stone stile to the right of a field gate. Go straight on with a row of mature trees on your right.

You will eventually meet a step-stile giving into a Woodland Trust area (Greendale Wood), where there are many new trees planted. Keep forward through this, above the site of Greendale Mill. Cross a footbridge and climb on the other side. As the gradient eases, the track forks. Bear right through more new plantings to emerge onto a lane near the Duke of York pub to complete the walk.